Contents:

Fold-out Insert: Panoramic of Old San Juan

2.	Map Puerto Rico	40.	La Cueva Del Indio, Arecibo
3.	Introduction	41.	Los Tubos, Manatí
4.	Puerto Rico	42.-43.	Panoramic of Condado Beach
5.	Garita	44.	Al Jíbaro Puertorriqueño
6.-7.	Panoramic Arecibo	45.	La Fortaleza
8.	Vieque Night	46.-47.	Panoramic of Calle Fortaleza and Calle Cristo
9.	Culebra	48.	Ferry Leaving Culebra Dock
10.	Castillo San Cristobal	49.	Mar Chiquita, Manatí
11.	Old San Juan	50.-51.	Panoramic of Castillo San Felipe del Morro
12.	Paseo de Pared de Viejo San Juan	52.	Panoramic of Luquillo Beach
13.	Condado	53.	Blue Beach, Vieques
14.	Aerial with Escambron	54.-55.	Panoramic of Paseo Lineal, Bayamón
15.	Castillo San Felipe Del Morro	56.	Aerial of Old San Juan with Cruise Ships
16.	Horses run wild in Vieques	57.	Crash Boat Beach, Aguadilla
17.	Aerial of San Juan's Urban Sprawl	58.	Vanderbilt Hotel
18.	Aerial of Condado & Ocean Park	59.	Christ Chapel
19.	El Yunque National Forest	60.-61.	Castillo San Cristobal
20.	Isabel II, Vieques	62.	Mangroves
21.	Ponce Fire House	63.	Map Culebra
22.	The Caribe Hilton	64.-65.	Flamenco Beach Panoramic
23.	El Yunque National Forest	66.	Castillo San Felipe del Morro
24.	Camuy Cave	67.	Plaza Roman Baldorioty de Castro, Juana Diaz
25.	Hato Rey	68.-69.	Los Morrillos Light, Cabo Rojo
26.	Benjamin Noriega Airport, Culebra	70.	Guanica State Forest Coastal Area
27.	Aerial view of Castillo San Felipe del Morro	71.	Mother-in-law's Pincushion
28.	Aerial of Condado & Ocean Park	72.	Los Canales, La Parguera
29.	Las Mareas	73.	Playa Caracoles, La Parguera
30.	Isla Verde Beach	74.	Canal in Culebra
31.	Arecibo with Observatory	75.	Beach Caracoles La Parguera
32.	Night Isla Verde Beach	76.-77.	Isla Verde Beach, La Perla
33.	Vieques	78.	Aerial old San Juan's
34.	Sentry post & Fortaleza	79.	Map Viequez
35.	Luquillo Beach	80.-81.	Media Luna Beach, Vieques
36.	Culebra Ferry Dock	82.-83.	Old Sugar Pier in Esperanza, Vieques
37.	View from Mt. Britton El Yunque National Forrest	84.-85.	Conde El Mirasol Isabel Segunda, Vieques
38.	Coqui	86.	Ocean Park
39.	Las Pelas, Culebra	87.	Iguana
		88	Map of Caribbean

ALL RIGHTS RESERVED UNDER INTERNATIONAL AND PAN-AMERICAN COPYRIGHT CONVENTIONS. NO PART OF THIS PUBLICATION MAY BE REPRODUCED, STORED IN A RETRIEVAL SYSTEM, OR TRANSMITTED IN ANY FORM OR BY ANY MEANS, ELECTRONIC, MECHANICAL, PHOTOCOPYING, RECORDING OR OTHERWISE WITHOUT THE PRIOR WRITTEN PERMISSION OF THE COPYRIGHT OWNER.

Designed and Published by Sunnyscene LLC
P.O. Box 7317, Reno NV 89510

www.sunnyscene.com
info@sunnyscene.com

© 2013 Mark Drenth
Photography © 2013 Mark Drenth
Inside Cover Pattern Design © 2013 Mark Drenth
Puerto Rico, Culebra, Vieques and Caribbean Maps
© 2013 Mark Drenth

Special thanks to Jay Zalduondo
for assisting the shoot in Culebra

Back of book: Green Beach

ISBN 10: 1-880760-61-4
ISBN 13. 978-1880-760-611

Library of Congress Control Number: 2013946437

Printed in China

Photos and Text by Mark Drenth

Puerto Rico

THE ISLAND OF ENCHANTMENT

Introduction

This book showcases many of the beautiful picturesque sites of Puerto Rico, La Isla Del Encanto or "Island of Enchantment". Puerto Rico is one of the Caribbean's top tourist destinations with thousands of visitors arriving each day by air and sea. Puerto Rico's beaches are world famous, as are her many historical sites, her cuisine, her nightlife and her year-round tropical weather. Tourists visiting Puerto Rico for the first time are amazed this island holds so many wonders. From the centuries old cobblestone streets of Old San Juan with it's massive forts, to the vast metropolis of San Juan; to the splendor of El Yunque National Forest and the offshore islands of Vieques and Culebra, it seems there is never enough time to see everything. Puerto Rico is an island with a long history dating back to the Spanish colonial days more than 500 years ago. Before that, many Amerindian groups inhabited Puerto Rico, the Taino Indians being the group the Spaniards encountered on their arrival to the island they called Borinquen. This book offers a small glimpse into the rich history and modern day Puerto Rico, including the many beautiful sites Puerto Rico has to offer, from air and land. By no means is this book intended to be a source for historical reference, but rather a showcase of striking images of the modern and historical Puerto Rico and related comments.

Puerto Rico

Originally named **Boriquen** by the Taino Indians, Puerto Rico was settled by several Indian groups long before Christopher Columbus visited it in 1493 on his second voyage to the New World. Christopher Columbus renamed Boriquen **"San Juan Batista"** and the island was given its present name, meaning "Rich Port" by Juan Ponce de Leon, who established a settlement inland from San Juan at Caparra in 1508. The Spaniards introduced sugarcane in 1511, and the first black slaves arrived in 1518. During the centuries that followed, the Spaniards concentrated on their richer colonies of Mexico and Peru. In the late 16th century the strategic value of Puerto Rico was realized and Spain began to fortify Puerto Rico, holding it against frequent English, Dutch and French attacks into the 19th century. Spain, which had granted almost complete autonomy to Puerto Rico by 1897, ceded the colony to the United States in 1898 after the Spanish-American war. The governor and legislature were federally appointed by the United States until 1917, when the **Jones Act** made all Puerto Ricans U.S. citizens and created an elected senate; however, Puerto Rico did not elect its own governor until 1948. Puerto Rico is located on the northern margin of the Caribbean Sea, east of the Dominican Republic and west of the Virgin Islands. A possession of the United States officially known as the **Commonwealth of Puerto Rico**, it encompasses 9,044 sq. km (3,492 sq. mi.) and has a population is 3,730.000. Until recently, such agricultural products as sugar, tobacco and coffee dominated the economy of Puerto Rico. **Operation Bootstrap** (1948) helped to transition Puerto Rico away from an agrarian economy to an industrialized economy. At present, employment in manufacturing, the service sector and tourism prevails. Puerto Rico is a rectangular island with an average north-south distance of 55 km (35 mi.) and east - west length that averages160 km (100 mi). In addition to the main island, the commonwealth includes several smaller nearby islands, including Vieques, Culebra and Mona. Puerto Rico's population is almost entirely of Hispanic origin with Spanish being the major language in Puerto Rico. English is now taught as a required second language and is widely understood by the people of Puerto Rico, although only a minority speaks it fluently. The overwhelming majority of the population are Christians, primary Roman Catholics.

A lonely garita or "sentry box" stands at a forward corner of **Castillo San Felipe del Morro**, also known as Fort El Morro. Over the years, the garitas have become icons of Puerto Rico, symbolizing Puerto Rico in print media distributed all over the world. Castillo San Felipe del Morro, which means **"Castle St. Philip of the Headland"**, was named after the patron saint of Spain's King Philip II. The fort is the older of the two main Puerto Rican forts that provided the sea and landward defenses, the other fort being Castillo San Cristobal. El Morro was begun in 1539 and served as Spain's defensive powerhouse to guard the entrance to San Juan bay. The open area in front of the garita is the moat, but was never filled with water. This was a dry moat, and covers the entire length of the landward side of the fort. The military reasoning for the moat was to be able to sink the main wall of the fort lower than ground level, providing El Morro with very high walls thereby making any attempt to scale the walls difficult. The moat also allowed the engineers to make the fort appear to have a low profile, thus providing attackers a 'smaller' target.

Panoramic Arecibo

This panoramic taken in Arecibo, shows the unique topography of Puerto Rico's mature karst countryside. Look to the center top of the panoramic to find the white suspension towers of the world famous *Arecibo Observatory*. Karst is one of the strangest types of rock formation in the world, it is characterized and formed by mildly acidic water that acts on carbonate rock, in this case limestone, and erosion over time contributes to larger and larger sinkholes, caves and underground rivers.

Stargazing in Vieques

With no distant city lights to obscure the night sky, stargazing in Vieques on a clear night can be a spectacular experience. The very long exposure of this photo exaggerates the dim lighting of this popular Vieques resort's pool area, leaving the observer to mistakenly assume the resort lighting would overcome any effort to stargaze, but the resorts night-lights are actually very dim and this does allow a fantastic view of the night sky, as seen in the photo.

Culebra

A short and inexpensive ferry ride from Fajardo, one can visit Puerto Rico's offshore island of Culebra. Sparsely populated, but sometimes overflowing with tourists, the island is held dear to all Puerto Rican's for its beauty and tropical white sand beaches. There are picturesque landscapes at seemingly every corner offering many photo opportunities. Culebra's system of paved and dirt roadways allow visitors to explore most of the island by car, or preferably a rented jeep. However, not all of Culebra is accessible even by jeep. Carlos Rosario, Resaca and Brava beaches, are accessible only by hiking or boating in.

Castillo San Cristobal

The vast green lawns of Castillo San Cristobal (visible on the right) show the different levels of the forts defenses. On the lower left of this photo is the white domed **Capitolio**, where the Puerto Rican government, specifically the House and Senate meet. The road going between the two structures leads to the entrance of Old San Juan.

Old San Juan

With the elaborately decorated wooden and iron grilled balconies, and the colorfully painted row houses lining cobblestone streets, the quaint magnetism of the Spanish colonial style architecture has become one of the main tourist attractions to Old San Juan. Even though many of the buildings are over 300 years old, careful renovations and strict building codes have maintained the original look of Old San Juan, offering the unique experience of exploring a 300 year-old preserved city.

Old City Wall Walk, Old San Juan

In 1680, the then governor of Puerto Rico, Enrique Enriquez de Sotomayer, began the construction of the city wall, a project that lasted almost 50 years. Today, the city wall remains one of the old world's architectural marvels, and offers a unique, incredible and well-preserved look at Spain's defensive foundation for Puerto Rico and the city of Old San Juan. During Spanish colonial times, most of the people who lived on the island, resided within the walls of Old San Juan.

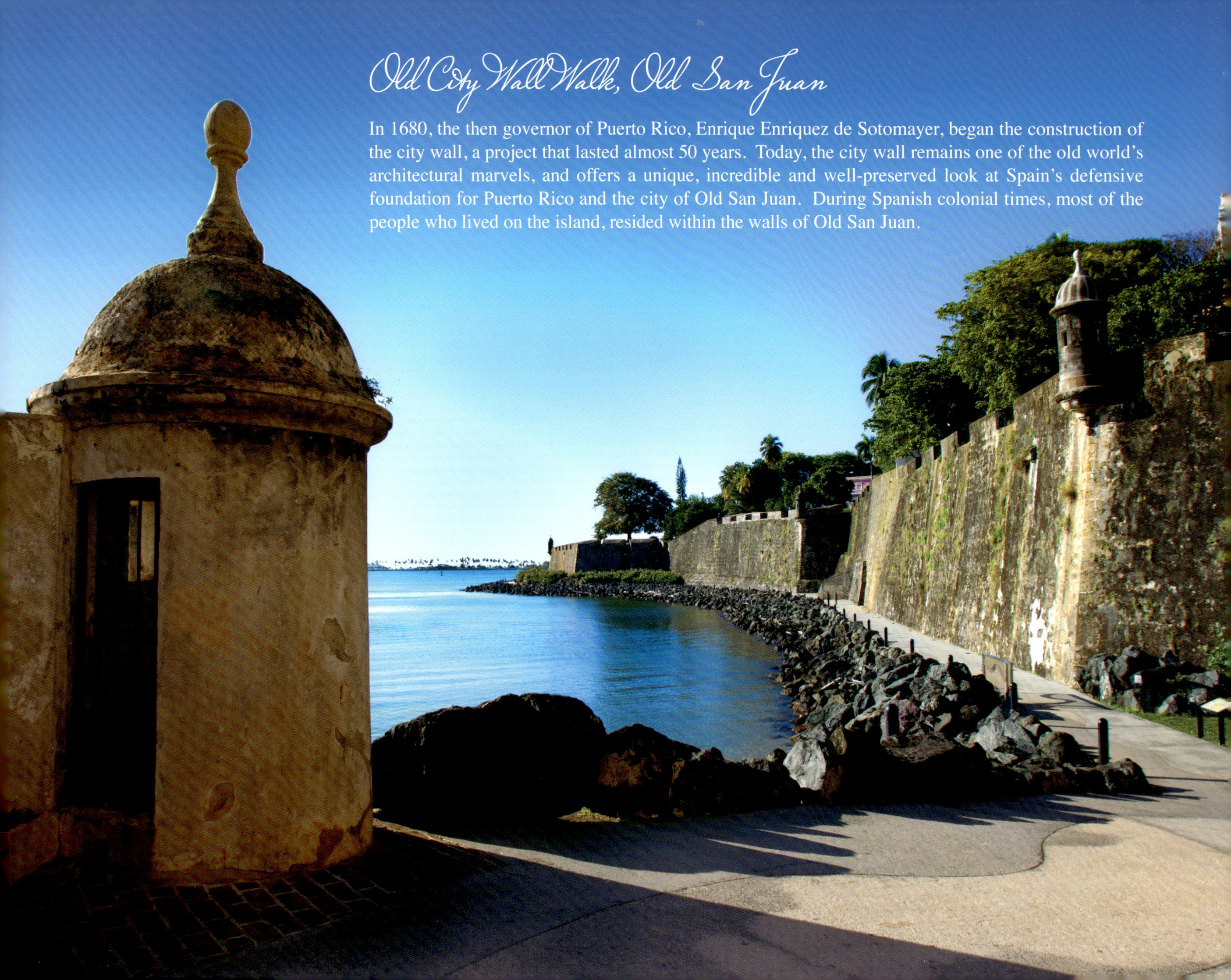

Condado

Originally planned at the turn of the century as an upper class neighborhood with large single-family homes, Condado today has transposed into a vibrant part of San Juan. Palm tree lined beaches offer a shady repose for those seeking sun and sand, while high-rise condos and luxury hotels line the beach.

Aerial with Escambron

An aerial with Escambron in the foreground and Isla Verde in the far distance. Playa Escambron, a Blue Flag beach, is visible on the bottom right of the photo. Playa Escambron is a family beach, offering a restaurant, changing facilities, lifeguards and restrooms. The beach is known for her calm waters due in part to the offshore coral reef (bottom right of photo) that shields the area from large waves. Elegant pedestrian walkways and bridges connect the beach with Parque Luis Munoz Rivera across the street. Parque del Tercer Milenio is located next to the beach, where one will find an exercise track and a multi-use stadium.

Castillo San Felipe Del Morro

Castillo San Felipe del Morro looking towards Old San Juan. The immediate building to the right with the red cupola is the University of Artes Plasticas, the premier art university in Puerto Rico.

Horses run wild in Vieques

Horses run wild in Vieques, and this can pose a problem while driving, and proper precautions must be taken. Sun Bay is one of many pristine beaches in Vieques, and directly in front of the beach are horse-grazing grounds (pictured).

San Juan's Urban Sprawl

An aerial view of San Juan's urban sprawl. The problems of urban planning and land use are apparent in San Juan, in part because most of the island's economic activity takes place there. During the early years of Operation Bootstrap (1942-1955), the side effect was an uncontrolled inflow of the population from other parts of the island and the concentration of industrialization in San Juan. The move away from an agrarian economy overwhelmed a city that was unprepared for so many re-locating. At the time, San Juan was where the ports and import/export infrastructures were located. Too much of the islands business was concentrated in San Juan. The government of Puerto Rico recognized this problem early and from the mid 1950's put in place a program of industrial decentralization, with the help of government incentives. The expressway cutting through the center of the photo is the Baldorioty de Casto, the main artery for travel between Luis Muñoz Marin International Airport and Old San Juan. In the distance, cruise ships docked in Old San Juan are visible, they are a crucial part of tourism for the island bringing with them a positive economic impact for the shops of Old San Juan.

Condado & Ocean Park

An aerial view looking east towards San Juan, Condado, Ocean Park and Isla Verde at the northern tip of the picture.

El Yunque National Forest

El Yunque National Forest is the only tropical rain forest in the US Forest System and covers some 28 thousand acres. Many rivers, streams and brooks can be found in El Yunque, this particular cascade in the photo is located on La Mina River, off of La Mina Trail. Day hiking the trails in El Yunque is one of the main reasons for visiting the national forest.

Isabel Segunda, Vieques

Six miles off the shore of Puerto Rico lies Vieques, and Isabel Segunda (photo) is one of two pueblos in Vieques, the other being Esperanza. Ferries from Fajardo leave throughout the day to Vieques, offering one of two ways to get to the island, the other being by air. Isabell II offers quaint restaurants, hotels, guesthouses, picturesque walks and attractions, including El Fortin Conde de Mirasol (the last fort the Spanish built in the new world) on the hill.

Ponce Fire House

Roughly an hour and a half drive from San Juan is Ponce, the second largest city in Puerto Rico. The city was named after the Spanish conquistador Juan Ponce de Leon. Located at the center of Ponce, in the town square *Plaza Las Delicias*, is the Parque de Bomabas. The Parque de Bombas was the cities fire station for 108 years, and in 1990 was converted into a fire-fighting museum. The iconic firehouse is now considered one of Puerto Rico's most notable buildings, and one will easily agree; the black and red horizontal stripes painted around the entire structure are quite memorable.

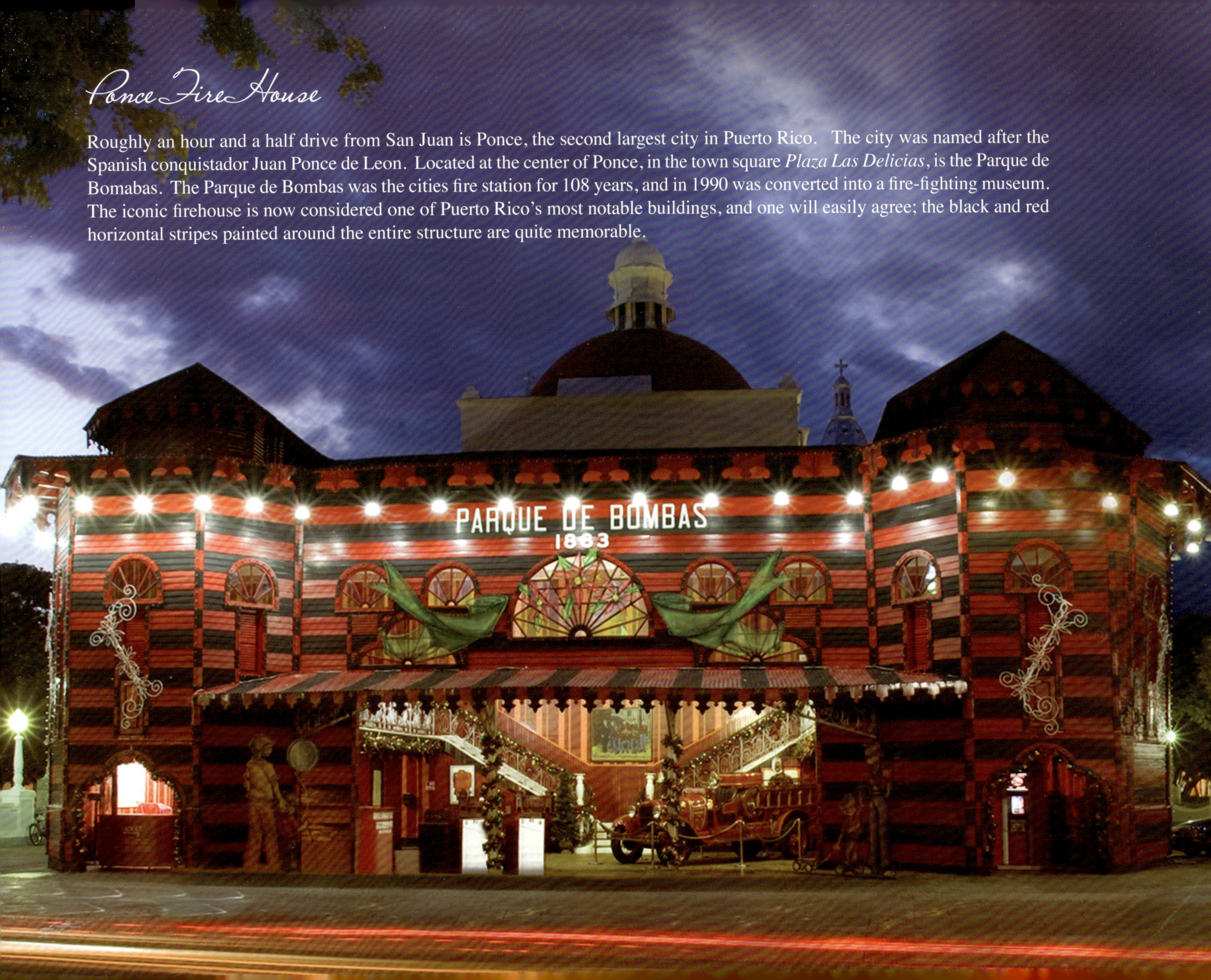

The Caribe Hilton

The Caribe Hilton holds a unique place in Puerto Rico's history. It's the hotel that popularized tourism to Puerto Rico, started Puerto Rico's upscale hotel building trend, (and arguably for the entire southern Caribbean) and kick-started tourism on the island. In the mid 1940's Puerto Rico began Operation Bootstrap, (an effort to attract big business in exchange for IRS tax incentives) to industrialize the island; thereby providing an alternative to the traditional agrarian economy of sugarcane plantations. In 1949, the government of Puerto Rico took the chance and designed, financed and built the hotel in Puerta de Tierra next to Fortin de San Geronimo, then put it out to bid, leasing the new hotel to Hilton Hotels. The spectacular Caribe Hilton was Hilton's first hotel located outside the continental United States. Puerto Rico's tourism industry was born, and during the deterioration of Cuban-American relations of the 1960's, offered a ready alternative to Cuba's sun and sand. The eventual Cuban embargo also helped Puerto Rico by inadvertently deflecting Cuba's American tourism industry to Puerto Rico. Over the years the hotel has undergone many renovations and expansions, continuing even today as of this printing. The original hotel from 1949 is still recognizable; it is the building to the left of the Hilton tower.

El Yunque National Forest

El Yunque National Forest, located in the **Sierra de Luquillo**, encompasses 28,000 acres and receives upwards of 200 inches of rain per year. It rains almost every day in El Yunque. El Yunque is home to rainforest flora and fauna, separated by distinct vegetation areas: **Tabonuco Forest, Palo Colorado Forest, Sierra Palm Forest** and the **Dwarf Forest**. El Yunque is also home to some of the most famous Puerto Rican animals including the **Puerto Rican Parrot**, the **Puerto Rican Boa**, and the **Coqui Frog**.

Camuy Cave

The Camuy River Cave Park, located in Camuy, is a large network of underground waterways and dramatic limestone caves, carved out by the third largest underground river in the world, the Rio Camuy. The cave system boasts more than 10 miles of caverns, and only a fraction of the system has been mapped to date.

Hato Rey

Located in Hato Rey are the headquarters of many local, federal and international businesses. Some of Hato Rey's residents include: insurance companies, government buildings, high-rise condominiums, the Jose Miguel Agrelot Coliseum, the FBI headquarters, and Puerto Rico's main banks among others. Locally known as The Golden Mile or Wall Street of the Caribbean, the area has been undergoing a transformation over the last decade to revitalize the area, the apparent focus being adding high-rise condominiums, urban train access and entertainment facilities.

Melones Beach, Culebra

First glance at Melones shrunken shore of rough rocky sand will turn many away, especially those looking for the idyllic white sugar sand fairytale Caribbean beach. Melones offers raw beauty, with Luis Pena Cay in the distance; picturesque Melones Beach is a metaphor for serenity. For many who visit Culebra, Melones Beach is their favorite, for that reason alone. Reading a book, snorkeling or just floating in the water are the popular activities at Melones. Melones being located on the west coast of Culebra brings another treat, colorful evening sunsets, animated even more so with Luis Pena Cay performing as an artist's backdrop.

Pueblo, Culebra

The main metropolis of Culebra is the sleepy town of Dewey, better known as **Pueblo**. Pueblo is also the island's sole community. Dewey is about ten minutes walk from the airport and it's also where the pier is located when arriving by ferry. Near the ferry dock is where one will find dive shops, cafes, guesthouses, bars, restaurants and the bank. Dewey was named after the victorious commander of the U.S. Asiatic fleet, Admiral George Dewey. A red and white structural steel drawbridge (pictured far left photo and right photo) is the only way across the canal that connects Bahia Sardinas where the ferry pier is located to the hurricane safe harbor of Ensenada Honda. The canal, which passes through Laguna Lobinas is where boaters can fill up their tanks and contract mechanical services. Crossing the bridge gives access to the southern portion of Culebra terminating with Punta Soldado. The panoramic canal photo was taken at the ever-popular **Mamacitas Guesthouse** restaurant and bar pier.

Ocean Park

Ocean Park and Condado, although famous for their tropical beaches are considered prestigious neighborhoods, where luxury residential high-rise condos and large ocean front homes are located. Condado is a mecca of restaurants, bars, clubs, coffee houses, upscale and boutique hotels, luxury shopping, and an all around popular entertainment district. In Condado, loitering is a fashion statement.

Las Mareas

Southeast of Salinas, off of route PR 703, is Las Mareas, a small fishing community whose residents live at the border of a mangrove forest and the Caribbean Sea. Local fishermen dock their "botes" or small boats, some colorfully painted, in a cove sheltered by distant mangroves that resemble small islands. By no means a tourist spot, Las Mareas does offer panoramic vistas, although it's off the beaten path.

Isla Verde Beach

Across the street from the Luis Munoz Marin International Airport is Isla Verde Beach. Lined by luxury hotels and high-rise condominiums, this palm-fringed tropical beach is considered one of Puerto Rico's more famous beaches, if not the most visited. Although there are no bars, clubs or restaurants directly on the beach, most hotels do have bars and restaurants located near the beach, on the hotel's private property for those staying at that hotel. Early morning joggers are also a common sight on the beach; the mornings offer those seeking beachfront exercise the tranquility of having the entire beach to themselves. For many, this is paradise.

Arecibo Observatory

The Arecibo Observatory is another famous Puerto Rican iconic structure recognized the world over; from a still cut-away in the first scene of 1969's Japanese **Gamera vs. Guiron** monster movie, to modern day Hollywood mainstream movies such as **Goldeneye** and **Contact**. For the movie going public, the message is simple; the iconic observatory represents a symbolic connection with "outer-space". The observatory, with a 1000 ft. diameter dish is the world's largest single aperture radio telescope. Built between 1960 and 1963, the telescope has gone through many technological upgrades over the years, and is currently operated under an agreement with the National Science Foundation by SRI International, Universities Space Research Association and Universidad Metropolitana de Puerto Rico. The observatory is tourist friendly, offering interesting and engaging science and astronomy exhibits, a science themed gift shop, a refreshment counter and outstanding observational areas to view the telescope.

Night Isla Verde Beach

Isla Verde beach, one of Puerto Rico's most treasured attractions for sun and sand, is arguably at its most spectacular during the evening, being indirectly lit up by the high-rise condominiums and hotels.

Vieques

Vieques is an idyllic tropical island, lying 8 miles off the east coast of Puerto Rico, which translates to 18 miles by ferry from Fajardo. Vieques is a favorite weekend destination for Puerto Ricans and is gaining popularity with mainstream tourists looking for an uncrowded, upscale but not too remote tropical getaway; the ferry ride from Fajardo only takes about 1 hour. Vieques is 21 miles long, 3 miles wide, encompassing 52 square miles, and acquired its name from the Taino word for 'Small Island'. Boasting some of the Caribbean's most sought after beaches, the island gained worldwide notoriety as the site of protests against the United States Navy's Vieques bombing range. This popular uprising, that also attracted international celebrities, led to the Navy's departure in 2003, and the conversion of the Navy's Vieques land into a wildlife refuge.

Sentry Post & Fortaleza

Attached to the city walls are garitas or 'sentry posts'. Here, a lonely garita overlooks **Paseo de la Princesa, La Fortaleza** and the **San Juan Gate**. The red door in the distance is the San Juan Gate, one of five original entrances into the old city, and unfortunately, the only one that remains. When the government demolished the eastern portion of the city wall near Castillo San Cristobal in 1897, they lost the Santiago Gate, which was the only gate that connected Old San Juan with the rest of the island. The other three rampart gates were **Puerta San Jose, Puerta Santa Rosa** and **Puerta de San Justo.** The walls of Old San Juan, the fortresses and La Fortaleza are a United Nations recognized **World Heritage Site.**

Luquillo Beach

Luquillo Beach, designated a Blue Flag Beach, is easily recognized by the rows upon rows of coconut palm trees and its crescent shaped beach. About 45 minutes from San Juan, the beach offers changing facilities, restrooms and refreshment stands. A favorite beach among locals and tourists alike, the beach normally offers a day of tranquility, with the exception of summer weekends and holidays. Camping is also allowed with a permit.

Culebra Ferry Dock

The ferry dock on the island of Culebra is small, but located in a convenient area within walking distance to shops, restaurants and hotels. The dock is located across the street from Dewey, Culebra's main town. Dewey itself covers only a few city blocks making it easy to get around on foot. Most day visitors to Culebra upon arriving there go directly to Flamenco Beach via taxi or, for a small fare, take a public (small bus). Interestingly, when **Culebrenses** (the native people of Culebra) cross the sound to the main island, the trip is referred to as "going to Puerto Rico", even though Culebra is itself a municipality of Puerto Rico.

Mt. Britton El Yunque National Forrest

At elevation 3,087 feet is the Mount Britton Lookout Tower, perhaps the parks most ambitious stone observation tower constructed. Built in the 1930's it is located after about a one-mile hike uphill through the Sierra Palm Forest. Once there, and if your lucky enough to have a break in the clouds, there are panoramic views of El Yunque, the Atlantic Ocean and the Caribbean Sea.

Coqui

A famous living cultural symbol of Puerto Rico is none other than the coqui, a small frog that sings loudly at night, making a sound that is similar to its name, "KOO-KEE". Scientifically, coquis belong to the **genus *Eleutherodactylus*** of which 16 different species live on the island. The 17th species, the Golden Coqui is believed to be extinct or critically endangered; no one has seen a Golden Coqui since 1981.

Las Pelas, Culebra

"Las Pelas" is located on Puerto Rico's off shore island of Culebra, and is a popular spot to drop anchor for the afternoon. In close vicinity is St. Thomas (background of this photo), one of the United States Virgin Islands and coincidentally, from a geological point of view, Culebra belongs to the Virgin Islands. The island cay on the top left is Culebrita, another very popular day sail destination. The dry subtropical landscape of Culebra pushes one to wonder if there is enough rainfall to supply the water needs of the residents who live on the small island. Strangely enough, the potable water supply is piped in from Vieques, and Vieques itself pipes in water from Puerto Rico.

La Cueva Del Indio

A picturesque sunset looking west from Arecibo's **La Cueva del Indio**.

Los Tubos

Los Tubos, located in Manati is one of Puerto Rico's better surf spots. The waves on this beach break in both directions, left and right. Los Tubos is also home to the Festival Playero, Manati's biggest yearly summer beach event.

Condado Beach

A Condado Beach panoramic, with the newly renovated La Concha Resort at center. The La Concha Resort, originally built in 1958, featured an architectural style known as the **Tropical Modernism Movement.** The resort today retains the essence of the original hotels architectural style only through the hard work of those who successfully fought to keep the original structure from being demolished. Today the luxury resort is a favorite among celebrities and tourists, and has remained an architectural icon of Puerto Rico. On the right of the panoramic, the twin buildings with the red tile roofs make up the recently renovated luxurious Condado Vanderbilt Hotel.

Jíbaro Puertorriqueño

On Puerto Rico Highway 52, at a rest stop on the southbound lane is a statue called ***"al Jibaro Puertorriqueno"***, built by the Government of Puerto Rico to pay respect to the Puerto Rican Jibaro. The 'Jibaros' were simple, hard working mountain folk that lived off the land, enjoyed playing and singing music but were also illiterate and uneducated. Some aspects of the Jibaro culture have over time become incorporated with modern day Puerto Rican culture, such as their work ethic, their enjoyment of all things musical (including their musical instruments), and even their hat, the ***pava,*** which was adopted as a symbol by the Puerto Rican political party PDP.

La Fortaleza

La Fortaleza or "The Fortress" was begun in 1532 and holds the unique honor of being the oldest executive mansion in continual use in the Americas. Since the 16th century, La Fortaleza has been the Puerto Rican Governor's residence, as well as host to various dignitaries such as President John F. Kennedy, Jacqueline Kennedy, King Juan Carlos of Spain and even President Obama, who visited the mansion for a short time during his day trip to Puerto Rico in 2011. La Fortaleza was originally built as a defensive structure, but there were reservations even before its completion regarding its poor strategic location. The army officers had informed the Spanish Crown it was being built "in a poor place", requested more money and soon started the impressive Castillo San Felipe del Morro. Today, La Fortaleza is a World Heritage Site as listed by UNESCO.

Calle Cristo

Calle Fortaleza and Calle Cristo

This 180 degree panoramic of Old San Juan covers two main streets, Calle Foraleza and Calle Cristo. In the distance on Calle Fortaleza is the streets namesake, the governor's mansion La Fortaleza. In the distance at the end of Calle Cristo is its namesake, Capilla de Santo Cristo. Capilla de Santo Cristo de la Salud, or better known as Cristo Chapel was built sometime around 1753 to honor a miracle, and help to prevent people from falling to their death over the city wall. The intersection of both of these streets showcases the colonial architecture restored to its original glory. It might be said that Old San Juan has never looked better.

Calle Fortaleza

Ferry Leaving Culebra Dock

The ferry from Culebra to the main island of Puerto Rico (and visa versa) takes about an hour and a half, the trip covering 17 miles with multiple departures throughout the day. There is also a cargo ferry albeit with a different departure schedule for those who would like to travel to Culebra with their own car, or have supplies to transport.

Mar Chiquita

Mar Chiquita is located on the north shore of Puerto Rico in Manati. The beach showcases a unique natural land formation, where a crescent shaped limestone wall with an opening to the open water lets small waves pass, yet also serves as a wave break for the larger waves. The limestone walls make a fun place to hike around, but can be dangerous if one is not careful.

Castillo San Felipe del Morro

This panoramic, taken from the forward portion of the Santa Barbara Battery of Castillo San Felipe del Morro, shows more detail and gives a perspective of the massive size of the fort. The Santa Barbara Battery, largest of all the harbor batteries, was the forth level of six levels of defense El Morro offered. The Santa Barbara Battery provided gunners with a high range of visibility; from here they used the canons to shoot at sails and rigging, destroying them with bar shot, split shot, and canister shot. The Carmen Battery, located at the top far left in front of the garita, was defense level five and protected the western sector of Old San Juan in addition to supporting the Santa Barbara Battery. Visiting El Morro offers a historical reminder of the power Spain wielded in the New World.

Panoramic of Luquillo Beach

Blue Beach

Blue Beach, also called "Playa Chiva", is located within the **Vieques National Wildlife Refuge**. To find this gem, one must venture a little deeper into the Wildlife Refuge; you could say it's off the beaten path, where the path is actually a broken down dirt road. Playa Chiva is uncrowded, rarely with more than a few people enjoying her white sand and calm swimmable waters. The beach is very long, and if divided into three segments, this photo is of the eastern most segment.

Paseo Lineal

Paseo Lineal, located in Bayamon alongside the upper bank of the Bayamon River, is one of Puerto Rico's hidden gems. The park follows 10 miles of the Bayamon River with two distinct paths, one only for bicycles, and the other for joggers, walkers or runners. The park is well maintained, and with all of the manicured lush tropical landscape, one might think Paseo Lineal was located within a botanical garden. Free of cost, abundant parking, plenty of security, restroom facilities, refreshment shacks, gravity exercise stations, and open from early morning until late evening, Paseo Lineal makes exercise seem like a walk in the park.

Old San Juan with Cruise Ships

One of the most popular ways to visit Puerto Rico, especially Old San Juan, is by cruise ship. Old San Juan is where Puerto Rico's main embark / debark piers are located and is generally the first place passengers arriving by cruise ship visit. Old San Juan is a paradise for those who prefer to explore on foot, as everything within the city walls is within walking distance. Easily recognizable landmarks and the streets laid out in a grid make it hard to get lost. Many cruise visitors, after experiencing a day in Old San Juan, make a point to someday return, spend more time and get to know the rest of the island.

Crash Boat Beach

Crash Boat Beach, easily accessible from the main roads, is another one of Puerto Rico's famous beautiful beaches. Located in Aguadilla, the name 'Crash Boat' came from its previous use as a military port, where rescue boats would patiently wait for downed aircrews from the (former) nearby **Ramey Air Force Base**, now the Rafael Hernandez Airport. Many colorful fishing boats are always lined up on the beach, ready for fishing at a moments notice. Scuba divers also rate this beach highly for its clear water, easy beach/shore access, and the abundant sea life found near and around the piers pylons.

Condado Vanderbilt Hotel

Began in 1917 and completed in October 1919, the Condado Vanderbilt Hotel was the first luxury hotel to open in Puerto Rico. Built at a cost of one million dollars by Frederick William Vanderbilt, the son of William Henry Vanderbilt whose father was Cornelius Vanderbilt, the railroad tycoon. Warren and Whitmore, the foremost architectural firm of the time, following Vanderbilt's request, utilized a 'Spanish Revival' architectural style for the hotel. One of the hotels original highlights, the entryway sweeping staircases, have been restored to their original grandeur and are shown in photo. During the 1970's, with the hotels popularity in decline and in need of renovation, the hotel was almost demolished, but a push to save the hotel and its architectural heritage was granted by an executive order by Governor Luis A Ferre declaring the property a cultural heritage.

Christ Chapel

Built in 1753, ***La Capilla del Cristo*** is a small chapel located at the end of Calle Cristo, built on the edge of the city wall. The 'legend' (there are a few) surrounding the chapel's construction tells of a young rider named Baltasar Montanez, who during June of 1750, while racing his horse during the festival of St. John the Baptist, was unable to make the turn at the end of Calle Cristo and fell over the edge. Normally this would lead to death, but Don Tomas Mateo Prats, prayed to Christ for salvation and a miracle occurred, Baltasar lived. The chapel was built in memory of the miracle and named "La Capilla del Cristo de la Salud". In another version of the legend, Baltasar dies, and to prevent more deaths, the chapel was built.

Castillo San Cristobal

Castillo San Cristobal or "St. Christopher Castle" is located about a mile east of El Morro and is the largest of San Juan's forts. While El Morro's main purpose was to protect the San Juan harbor, fort San Cristobal's main purpose was to protect Old San Juan from attacks approaching from the eastern landside as well as the eastern area of sea. The need for the fort and the vulnerability of El Morro was shown on two occasions, once when in 1598 the Earl of Cumberland's English troops attacked El Morro by coming through Old San Juan, and in 1625 when the Dutch attacked from the same direction. The fort was begun in 1634 and took on its present shape during the main years of its construction, 1765- 1783, when Chief Engineer Thomas O'Daly

and later Juan Mestre were in charge. San Cristobal was the largest fortress built by Spain in the New World, covering about 27 acres, and sealing the eastern entrance to Old San Juan with an impressive set of double gates. The fort served its purpose by repelling in 1797 Sir Ralph Abercromby's unsuccessful attack with an estimated 7,000 British troops. About a third of the fort was demolished in 1897 in an effort to expand Old San Juan. Today Castillo San Cristobal is a part of the San Juan National Historic Site.

Mangroves

Puerto Rico has a number of coastal mangrove habitats, the most famous being La Parguera in Lajas, but they are also found in Vieques and Culebra. Mangroves grow in the tropics and subtropics in the sediments of coastal seawater, specifically where sediments can accumulate over time in areas where wave energy does not wash the sediments away. Mangrove swamps are also common in Puerto Rico, such as the image above, taken in Las Mareas, an area south of Salinas. Las Mareas offers coastal mangrove habitats and mangrove swamps, but unlike La Parguera, they are not a tourist attraction. Here, they are just a calm place for local fishermen to fish. Mangrove areas provide a degree of protection from erosion and storm surges during hurricanes due to their massive root systems, which in turn provide ecosystems for coastal sea life enabling even more sediment to be trapped.

Flamenco Beach

Culebra's fabled Flamenco Beach as seen from the old abandoned military observation post on the hill. Flamenco Beach is undoubtedly one of the main reasons tourists visit Culebra; considered one of the world's most beautiful beaches by magazines and television, this half mile stretch of tropical white sugar sand sits in a crescent shaped stretch of coastline, and offers calm swimmable water in a beautiful setting that is rarely crowded. On some parts of the beach the sand bar continues far into the bay, one can walk a hundred feet out into the water and only be knee deep.

Ground View, Flamenco Beach

This panoramic view photographed from one of several entrances to the fabled Flamenco Beach was taken on a crowded day and offers a better perspective of the beach's size. For those who make the trek to Culebra, Flamenco Beach is the most famous, but not the only beautiful beach in Culebra. A few of the other notable beaches on Culebra include Resaca, Zoni, Brava, Culebrita, Carlos Rosario, Malena, Tamarindo and Punta Soldado.

Castillo San Felipe del Morro

From this aerial view, one can see the various levels of El Morro's defenses. The most forward battery and the first level of defense was the Water Battery located at almost sea level. Canon balls fired from this level could skip across the water and punch holes in the vessel's waterline area. The second level of defense was the Tower, located behind the Water Battery. The third level of defense was the Casemate Guns; these faced seaward and offered gunners the added protection of bombproof casemates, or gunrooms. The fourth level of defense was the Santa Barbara Battery; this battery was the largest and encompasses the deck of the forward portion of El Morro. Defense level five included the canons located at the Carmen Battery; these guns protected the western section of Old San Juan and provided additional backup to the Santa Barbara Battery. The Hornwork was the sixth level of defense; the canons pointed toward Old San Juan, thus protecting El Morro from a land attack.

Plaza Roman Baldorioty de Castro, Juana Diaz

Located in the town center of Juana Diaz is the beautiful and traditional town plaza, **Plaza Roman Baldorioty de Castro.** The plaza was rebuilt and opened in 1996 utilizing the original designs from the 1960's thereby preserving the heritage and spirit of the original Juana Diaz town center. Construction of the neo-classical structure **San Ramon Nonato Parish Catholic Church** at the center of the plaza began in 1813, and construction of the church's two towers began in 1870.

Los Morrillos Light, Cabo Rojo

Perched upon a coastal cliff is the Cabo Rojo Lighthouse, a favorite place for those who enjoy watching a colorful sunset. The lighthouse, located at the southwestern tip of Puerto Rico, was built in 1882 by the Spaniards to assist passing ships through the Caribbean Sea through the dangerous Mona Passage into the Atlantic Ocean. Los Morrillos Light, a beautiful example of Spanish colonial architecture, is located at the edge of a 200 feet high limestone cliff, surrounded by salt-water lagoons and marshes. Although the lighthouse has been abandoned for years, the light is still in operation.

Guanica State Forest Coastal Area

The Guanica State Forest, located on the southwestern coast of Puerto Rico covers about 10,000 acres, and is a United Nations Biosphere Reserve. Unlike El Yunque National Forest, Guanica State Forest is a dry subtropical forest, receiving only about 30" of rain per year. Prickly-pear cactus dot the landscape of this dry forest, providing contrast to Puerto Rico's image of palm tree lined sugar sand beaches. For the tourist, the Guanica State Forest offers miles of nature trails winding through its rough landscape, making for an interesting day of exploring and sightseeing.

Mother~in~law's Pincushion

Melocactus intorus, also known as Turk's Cap Cactus, Mother-in-law's Pincushion and Barrel Cactus is native to Puerto Rico and other Caribbean Islands. Turk's Cap Cactus is found in the coastal limestone areas, as seen here in this example from the coastal area of Guanica State Forest.

Los Canales, La Parguera

Cays and Islets of mangrove trees located off the coast of Lajas form the basis of La Parguera. Of the many activities available in Pargurea, visiting 'Los Canales' or 'The Canals' are among the most popular. The canals are easily reached by any number of local vendors located at La Pargurea, whose offerings range from the rental of a kayak to guided tours on flat-bottomed boats. The canals are an extensive system of man made narrow waterways through the mangrove formations, said to offer shelter for watercraft during hurricanes. Exploring the canals can be a confusing experience unless one is familiar with the terrain.

Playa Caracoles, La Parguera

Caracoles beach is one of the few beaches where there is no physical beach. Water enthusiasts flock to Playa Caracoles daily in boats, kayaks and jet skis to spend the day at this popular Parguera hangout, wading in the calm shallow water soaking up the sun's rays. One of the enjoyable activities at the Caracoles cay is swimming through the mangrove canal, taking a break from the sun and observing the sea life in the mangrove's roots. No longer a sleepy fishing village, day or night, La Parguera is a popular tourist spot offering restaurants, hotels, bars and nightlife for those looking to enjoy time off.

Benjamin Noriega Airport

The offshore island of Culebra makes a wonderful weekend getaway from the fast pace and traffic of San Juan. For those who wish to get their by air, the island's Benjamin Noriega Airport (CPX) offers regularly scheduled and reasonably priced flights from Old San Juan's Isla Grande airport and Ceiba's airport near Fajardo. Ensenada Honda Bay in the background is a popular drop anchor spot for sailboats due to the protection it offers from hurricanes and choppy water.

Kill the Cat

Mata La Gata or 'Kill the Cat' is a unique small mangrove cay (roughly 1500 x 1200 feet) in the Parguera Nature Reserve, accessible via a short boat or kayak ride from La Parguera. Kill the Cat cay is a recreational area, resembling a miniature park, having a picnic area with BBQ's, an extensive wooden boardwalk through the cay's mangroves for nature observation (photo), a restroom and changing facilities, and an ocean pool. Surrounding the cay is the crystal clear calm tropical water that has made La Parguera famous. Ocean encounters with sea creatures, such as starfish, sea cucumbers, fish, dolphins and turtles are common, adding to the many attractions of La Parguera.

Panoramic Isla Verde Beach

La Perla

Much has been written about La Perla, a shantytown built along the battlements that connect Castillo San Cristobal to Castillo San Felipe del Morro. Colorful shacks, appearing to be stacked one on top of the other, have given the Puerto Rican government their fair share of problems over the years. Problems with drugs, violent crime and general lawlessness has cast a dark shadow over La Perla, a strange contrast to the tourist friendly reputation the government has established for the rest of Old San Juan.

Aerial of Old San Juan

Prominently displayed at the forefront of Old San Juan is the Governor's mansion La Fortaleza. Old San Juan, with her barely navigable grid of narrow yet heavily trafficked streets has for centuries been the heart of Puerto Rico. That said, the narrow streets have not constricted the continued growth of Old San Juan. Even today, the old city beats steadily onward, in an evermore-lively manner, housing various universities, two impressive forts, art galleries, museums, shops, plazas, churches, fine restaurants, a brewery, the cruise ship piers, in addition to being the home of Puerto Rico's governor.

Paradise Found at Media Luna Beach, Vieques

Media Luna Beach, located within the Vieques National Wildlife Refuge is to most visitors the definition of paradise found. Media Luna is the first beach after Sun Bay Beach, accessible via the dirt road that winds through the Wildlife Refuge. Sand bars extend out into the bay, beckoning those who even suffer from aquaphobia to enter and enjoy her warm tropical splendor. A trip to Vieques will unite you with other fastidious beach connoisseurs, those who travel to destinations specifically to visit a particular beach, over and over again. Why? Because these pristine Vieques beaches have been

off limits to the general population for 62 years, in effect, frozen in time, undeveloped. Red beach, Green Beach, Blue Beach as with the other beaches on the old Navy's land have been inaccessible to the public since 1941, when the Navy expropriated two thirds of Vieques. In 2003 the Navy left the eastern end of Vieques, transferring the land, which in turn became the Vieques National Wildlife Refuge.

The Old Sugar Pier in Esperanza, Vieques

Sugarcane plantations and their corresponding mills formed the principal economy of Vieques from the mid 1800's until the industries collapse in the 1940's. Sugar piers and railways were built to expedite the sugar quickly from the mills out to ships for export. The names of the sugar mills were

eventually adopted as the town names, such as Esperanza, Puerto Real, Playa Grande and Santa Maria. The depression of the 1930's led to the closure of all but one of the sugar mills, Playa Grande, which itself eventually closed when the Navy set up operations on Vieques.

Panoramic from El Fortin Conde Mirasol, Vieques

El Fortin Conde de Mirasol has the unique honor of being the last military fort built by the Spaniards in the western hemisphere. The Spaniards decided to colonize Vieques during the mid-1800's and in 1843 the municipality of Vieques was established. Today, the fort is impeccably well maintained and preserved, housing a museum of Viequenese Art and history. The fort was built between 1845 and 1855 by orders from the Count of Mirasol, the then

governor of Puerto Rico to provide protection from British and Danish attacks. El Fortin Conde de Mirasol offers a panoramic view of the town Isabel Segunda.

Ocean Park

Mild waves and a pleasant strip of wide tropical sand greet those who visit Ocean Park Beach, located between Condado and Isla Verde. Known locally as "the" beach to see and be seen. Boutique hotels line the beach, most with upscale beachside restaurants and bars.

Tree Chickens in Puerto Rico

Iguanas are not native to Puerto Rico, and have become a nuisance, chewing up crops, burrowing under roads and affecting the ecosystem. There are more iguanas than people in Puerto Rico, in part because Puerto Ricans never acquired a taste for eating them, unlike other Latin American countries where iguana meat is a delicacy found in the local recipes.

Puerto Rican Holidays Guide

January 1	New Year's Day
January 6	Three King's Day
2nd Monday in January	Eugenio Maria de Hostos' Birthday
3rd Monday in January	Martin Luther King's Birthday
3rd Monday in February	Presidents Day
March 22	Emancipation Day
Good Friday	The Friday before Easter
Easter	Easter occurs on the first Sunday following the first full moon that occurs on or after the first day of spring (vernal equinox).
3rd Monday in April	Jose de Diego's Birthday
2nd Sunday in May	Mother's Day
Last Monday in May	Memorial Day
3rd Sunday in June	Father's Day
July 4	United States Independence Day
3rd Monday in July	Luis Munoz Rivera's Birthday
July 25	Puerto Rico Constitution Day
July 27	José Celso Barbosa's Birthday
1st Monday in September	Labor Day
October 12	Columbus Day
November 11	Veterans Day
November 19	Discovery of Puerto Rico Day
4th Thursday in November	Thanksgiving Day
December 25	Christmas Day